W0007426

ZEN STRINGS

The Ways of a Music Disciple

HARRY MORAGA

ZEN STRINGS

ZEN STRINGS

Copyright © 2015 Harry Moraga

Edited by

Valery Glod & Shanna Moraga

Cover Art by Rebecca Magnoni

Interior Lotus Andrew Maclean

Printed in USA

ISBN 9781515111733

Table of Contents

Introduction

Anything that people do with extraordinarily focus and persistent vitality, whether it be music, sports, academics or life in general, can surprise us with mysterious, unexpected epiphanies. I really wanted to explore the external and internal perceptions of my personal growth practicing, studying, obsessing and understanding the self-medication that comes with a creative mind. The lifelong voyage I chose began with a different expectation than that of the present truth by which I have been educated by. I hope to share my own experiences, expose the fruits of a "tragedy to triumph" story, and uncover some common ground.

Perceptions

Theory is like a river of white dye, distinct and calculated in its essence, but also the foundation to the chemistry that can give birth to the rainbow of originality. May we wander through the stream and bleed the colors of our reality.

Intervals and patterns within modal constructs should be played with while being rearranged. The sense of adventure and "newness" will come from an unfamiliar place that dwells within the confines of a scale. Know the steps but move left and right of them to tread your own trail.

If an application is not known to you, study it for a moment, its rhythms and its fundamentals. Incorporate knowledge you've accumulated into your creative goals. Why collect all the fish at once when your need to hunt and your perception of taste will always progress?

Confusion in your own artistry and work can be a derivative of a higher level of intuitive, unconscious creativity. Allow these moments of uncertainty to weigh themselves out. Your decision in the end will feel clear and the critical voice will slip away. This can be a sign of creativity harnessing our skills and imposing upon us, at the present moment, a new level of ability. Let's allow it to be an eccentric feeling that suggests the idea of trusting ourselves.

Come prepared when sitting in a group session. Ideas don't always manifest themselves through the party. Bring material that has thought in its roots but is vulnerable in its foundation. It needs to remain loose to the collective consciousness. Your consistent effort to contribute to your community will forge a productivity that can enhance the level of craft in your songs. It will also seal the sense of devotion towards yourself and your members. Your efforts will be looked at as belief in the group's ambitions and work.

There is a great fear of sacrifice when pursuing any muse that can require companions. We can come across characters who cannot undertake the shedding of perpetual comforts. As these relationships move in and out of our lives, certain setbacks can grind away the faith in achievement. But it's an honor to contribute towards the imaginative arena that inspires societal shifts. When certain companions lack the legs to travel the distance for which you've trained tirelessly for, may yours carry you to someone else with legs alike.

There is an analogy that we use for our guitars by calling it an "axe". Try rethinking that idea with the concept of a loyal horse. It has a body, a neck and an upper section that resembles a saddle. Think of writing your song as a battle and your guitar the mighty stead you've chosen to ride in on. Your guitar goes through the same bumps and bruises you endure trying to assemble something worth listening to. It will always ride in with your optimism and carry you out in your glory or failures. Just as you do, your "horse" will gain strength and wisdom with the completion of each battle and every war it rides away from.

Humor the idea that music isn't everything but everything is music. If music were everything, there would be no value in translating anything into music. However, because of its symbolic, all-inclusive nature, anything can be expressed using the language of music. From heartache in relationships and opinions cemented in belief, to the awe-inspiring sight of an atom. The mind is the medium that connects everything to music, which is the bridge that links us all.

When we worry about the fear in how like-minded listeners will point their focus towards our art, know that that is always a fool's game. We, as creators, will always employ techniques and themes, learned from our teachers, and then translate them into something new, making them our own. When you pull from your influences, you become reminiscent of your influences. Those who enjoy your teacher's works, will surely lend a curious ear to your translations and interpretations.

There is an aspect of being an artist that can feel like it comes with a hefty price. Our interpretations and self-discernment are always magnified. We feel life with an overwhelming sense. To translate what we feel and see into art, we seem to always monitor life with great depth. With this great depth can come with this inability to cope or understand ones emotions without using ones art as a catharsis. Identity in your craft can be a terrifying water to tread. Still, feel fortunate that you live a life by the mirror sword of self-reflection. Because of the hypersensitivity in your perspectives, everyday common situations are transformed into unique situations. The intensity of your analysis may just be deeper layers of an environment which you have yet to tap or understand.

There's an old teaching in the Zen discipline which describes the aspect of being a "watcher", emotionally detached from your own sense of self and personality. You can condition empathy and patience by playing the role of the observer. The lesson can be applied when you're working with a group of musicians. Some people, particularly musicians, tend to run heavily on the ego. The ego collects opinions, beliefs and phenomenon about truth and falsehoods. This, later on, can build a stubborn and inflated sense of self. Have patience in your fellow musician because we all only know what we've allowed ourselves to accept. Have empathy for your fellow musician because they also may be running on the momentum towards gratification and glory through their craft. Mold yourself around the different entities surrounding you and be the unity within the differences. Be like water, my friend.

Isolation is an animal that one should embrace. It has great potential to morph the mind in many wild directions. That is why some of the greatest inspirations can come when one is alone. They are the moments when absolute discipline can be imposed by unconditional ambition. Unbalanced thinking or melodramatic distractions should be eradicated and the straight, tightrope in front of you should have your full attention. By any means necessary, divert the selfishness of standing with idle hands. Instead, show the hands how to steer one's life and grasp at the helm.

There are many spells that can be confusing and productive all at once. The heaviest load to bear can be the spell of obsession. So much beauty that occurs on the search for creative heights can be shadowed by the kiss of addiction. The mind and the body we support are stirred through a variety of experience and interactions. Be wary of the obstacles you place in front of your potential. Do not only allow one creative option for an infinitely creative mind. If, for example, one puts down the guitar and picks up a martial art, the focus and discipline might expand to different and undiscovered realms of potential. There are many rewards and losses to witness when spearheading another pursuit. Learning the intricacies within other artistries induces a process that flexes and tests the musical mind, which empowers it with a vitality only found when stimulated by another way of problem solving. The energy given to music can transcend to the martial art and possibly return again to the music. Without expanding the concentration, you'll never know the potential of one discipline. In the end there is a great possibility they will enhance each other.

The second guessing that the mind can present itself with is one of the musician's greatest adversaries. A song, a riff, an idea can be completed but once the novelty of it has been overly intellectualized, the idea becomes clouded with anxiety and self-doubt. The mind can second guess its creativity by building a false sense of perspective that it believes could be the "listener" or potential audience. We must have confidence in ourselves and our work to avoid getting tangled by our own misapprehensions. Discard the false outlook that in the end will hinder and dismantle your road to progress. You can only represent yourself. You do not have the ability to feel or think on any others behalf about whether or not your ideas, as an artist, are valuable or not. Most intuitive thoughts are extensions of our deep insights and insight is the fish that the net of art desires.

Through history, by innovation, man has evolved through moments of self-reflection and surveillance. Water to mirrors, stories to sound bites and photo to video have all, but not exclusively, been tangible tools towards a modern day approach of self-analyzing. We now have the chance to document our thoughts, capture our emotional tides and reflect upon our imagination and action. Within many circles there are two dueling opinions amongst musicians. The first idea is about the artist who enjoys moving on to the next creation after it has been completed. The other is that of the artist who only enjoys her creation in the moment without any regard to the completion or how it's received by anyone. In this day and age it would benefit a certain amount of us to study ourselves, to understand ourselves. Artists may cringe at the sound or sight of their own outdated performances, thinking that they have surpassed that moment. What can be taken into consideration should be the fragments in those previous works that capture the essence of the practitioner's intention. With every new song the writer digs to uncover his vision and with every song, they leave behind clues and impressions of that vision. Use the tools of observation. Be one with the idea that foolish moves can be accompanied by decisive ones. It is to our advantage to look backwards to pinpoint and connect those breakthroughs that fuel our principle while moving forward. Technology may be a double edged sword best held by its handle.

The way in which a painter provokes contemplation and an athlete inspires fortitude is how the musician should approach his work. When sitting in the soundscape of music, a listener can be internally transformed and emotionally influenced. The translation of music has aided individuals in penetrating their personal walls of turmoil as well as calling the collective towards the entities of a negative opposition. Whether the musician is aware of it or not, they have the potential to be a catalyst for endless, internal revolutions amongst the mindful ear. The reach an artist has with her intent should reflect from her service inward that both weigh heavy with honesty. In how a journalist digs for truth and exploits the reality is how a musician should discover their own and portray it passionately.

There's a personal quality that most ambitious people have. It's the rope that pulls at the waist of the struggling heart. It's all empowering and infinite in its depth. It is self-motivation. Some of us feel gratified when given praise for our work. It can fuel us to contribute and contrive to our objectives. But if the other side of that were to occur, and recognition were to be replaced with criticism, paralysis of the mind may ensue. The focus toward negativity can weigh much more than its counterpart. One point of view may be to devalue the positive reinforcement. Some musicians can find a more consistent motivation when they don't rely on external praise. To drive the concentration in the direction of a place that doesn't magnify on the good that people chatter about can condition the perceptive scope on the reaction to the other malevolent judgments. Emptiness beyond the phenomenon, the duality of black and white can be a moving dictation of motivation. You choose how, when and why, never them.

Our actions at times can be manipulated by layers upon layers of opinions. We may do and say things solely based around our ever changing belief systems. Imagine deconstructing the view towards your creative process, your moments of improvisation. Like the evolution of a caterpillar, the mind can shed its previous form. Picture yourself in darkness and as you move around you seem to step on something reminiscent of an insect. For a moment one can feel squeamish even remorseful. As you turn the light on, you find that what you had crushed was merely a dried maple leaf. Thoughts can find a way to snowball through logic and out of reality. Use this example to contemplate that if you enter your creative zone knowing the mind can mistake itself, be critical towards your habitual discriminations. The way in which the insect was the mistake may also be like the comfortable and accustomed stroke of your brush to the canvas. Explore unacquainted territory. Bear some resistance and deconstruct.

Moments of sheer terror over an obligation you've agreed to with yourself to show, speak or perform your abilities in the public eye can stir and surface the anxious thought. Discuss within and to others in a way that suggests calm and confidence about the situation, against all worrying influences. The fear of a situation that doesn't exist yet is inflated by the stressful projection of failure. A simple positive assumption can influence the intuitive energy you will give off during the moment of a premeditated performance. Convince yourself of the success in the unknown and link the instinctual spark through the doubt and to the moment by moment action. Avoid the mental hiccups by assuring yourself of a decisive outcome at all costs.

As we enjoy music and many other things, we construct the system to why we enjoy it. The basis to our argument is built with the bricks of pre-exposed labels and conditional characteristics like image, sound, content and genre. After our tower of taste has been achieved, opposition becomes offensive in the form of alterations and foreign ideas. The attachment to our "high horse" can inflate an aspect of our ego that identifies itself as an attribute of a purist. The purist is devolved, playing in his own courtroom that deals with the cases of linear tradition being threatened by new expanding ideas. Burn that court and its jury full of false discriminations that oppose innovations! Declare anarchy to all who stand on the backs of adventurous inventors! Chop at the tower and demand that the chimp turn into a man and man into the future!

In engineering the weapon of influence with all its tangible, perceptible forms, somewhere we should contemplate that these results may be a byproduct of something with very powerful and tamable traits as is the great ego. To draw a painting, write a book or compose a song, the artist has at some point come to terms that what they do is validated by them themselves and knowing they have more to give of value enough to place it in a public space. There are those who believe in erasing the ego entirely. But with no ego leaves a space of potential, unknown. How does an audience hear live music? How do motivating words drive a reader? The ego must be present in the preparation and execution. It can convince you to step away from being the observer and being the observed. Ponder, that ignoring the ego may cause it to bloat, but to recognize it is to command it and its dynamic quality.

No matter the amount of time one picks up his instrument, the guilt of not practicing enough scratches at the neck of many musicians. As a guitar player, the beginning stages are immersed in countless hours of analytical technique building. But as time passes some may concentrate more on the storytelling side of playing rather than the technical. Certain musicians gravitate to playing only when inspiration hits for a new song. But if these moments of creativity don't occur more often than we desire, the guilt of not working through a training session or focusing attention to any part of our work may unleash the facade that blinds the view of ourselves as a dedicated practitioner. A songwriter practices his craft by living and observing the events that move and pass through him. When they sit with their instrument, it's time for something to be said. Life pushes them to their guitars, pianos, drums. The instrument does not pull them. Leave guilt to the wind and know that only when your life moves so will it provoke you to move your strings.

There's a sword that cuts through impressions and shatters opposition. It's the blade that can separate the outcome of ignorance and cognizance, belief and non-belief. This is the katana of defiance. The world is constantly at work pushing trivial and pseudotraditional standards upon anyone in search for a line to stand in. The yearning for some type of certainty becomes a trap as your irrational emotions become the new intended target. Question information. Raise a brow to even your own consensuses. Investigate all influence because a ruling hand can tend to come from a deceptive sleeve. Defiance toward opinions and information does not need to be carried with an extremist strut but with an awareness so inexhaustible that the core of the illusions fear your presence.

Close your eyes for a moment. See yourself through the eyes of a mother and next, the eyes of a sister. Ponder that you may be many identities in perception but one in your true expression. Apply this transcendence in how we project the dimensions of music no matter the instrument. The sound, pitch, frequency and heart of music are void of all preference and partiality to the mediums of their manifestations. Try to discard the sonic characteristic of your primary instruments. Forget the swelling and stroking of a cello line. Forget the conventional attack towards guitar phrasing. Deconstruct the pulse and sway of a piano cadence. To engineer a creative moment around the surpassing of qualities an instrument holds can spring many untapped and experimental elements of your musical mind to fruition. Never contain yourself to stylistic boxes due to your instrumental circumstances. Let go of the habitual foundations and explore the stones beneath the sand.

If the mind is able to perceive three directions, past, present and future, can the past and future disrupt the present? Thoughtlessness may be one of many useful options. Plenty would advocate the irresponsibility of not considering the footsteps ahead and behind us. To push away and escape the systems where fear repeatedly forces the notions that are unknown unto us may aid in the progression and evolving of the near and now moment. The mind doesn't function when the mind is preoccupied with all of time but the current. Forget the past for only a blink. Calculate the power of the present. The effort now will complete the task later. Thoughtlessness can take the energy from the distraction of two mental movements and utilizes it in a productive channel when focused appropriately. Contemplate the present and be free to reinvent and represent yourself.

As real and as life changing the muses of creativity are, their boundlessness can attract oneself to achieve on unbalanced priority. As the ambition surfaces, its overwhelming importance becomes the tunnel through which the train of thought barrels down uncompromisingly. Certain aspects of a mindful, social life can be hindered with the lack of experience in properly presenting yourself and engaging others by the hand of a personal obsession. It can be a wonderful thing when a person is reflective and productive in times of concentration. But to disregard the many other aspects of a full life only to constantly try and fill the cup of dignity with the oils of recognition can become a damaging process. The constant movement and attack towards acceptance foils your strength to climb the vines of self-worth. Meditate with your craft so that you may not die by your craft. But if demise were to rise, your potential will have mourned your death.

The powerful undercurrent of attitude that flows throughout the day by day observation can reflect itself in the very form that modifies itself. That force, is music and its influence on occasional mental movements. We shape our environment at times to the type of music our deepest feeling calls for. Since the varieties of audible combinations are endless, there are handfuls that are bound to communicate with our moods and consolidate their complexities. As many students and listeners alike will agree, music carries a conspicuous therapeutic element to which the phenomenon of anger, happiness, sadness and their derivatives expose themselves in a palpable way. In the same way that our emotions pull us to bring them toward the surface with a musical motivation, it can also be equally influential by externally provoking the emotion and attitude through music. Try using it to maneuver the victories in your prospect.

Time is a permanent variable of life that ceases to stay the same. And as time sails the infinite, it carries us along only to expose our common law of impermanence and evolution. Blood cells, lunar cycles, behaviors and perceptions continually ascend towards change by the quality of movement supported by time. Disruption of personal progress can come from our static position in comfortable and familiar states of mind. Those moments of stand-still are the spaces where confusion, doubtfulness, anxieties and pain can dwell. The idea is to move your mind with a different approach and break through the resistance that is "old thinking." Our pain can remind us to step off the train tracks and move up and over the rails from the impending destruction. When blood stops its flow, life becomes compromised. When a musical approach has been exhausted, the execution process is infiltrated with certain angles of repetitiveness. When we've unintentionally hurt the hearts around us, our awareness of the change in our relationships has become diminished. Many aspects of conscious life require the ability to adapt, whether it's in the empty well of creativity or perceptive development of the character in a malleable man. Flow with the harmony of change to uphold the continually expanding discoveries of self.

Since most musical minds have a constant rotation of ideas and melodies bouncing around, try to use silence as the capturing net. Our days and nights can be engulfed in music through many mediums which initially may be the very tool for our inspiration. But to drive in silence, walk in silence and sit in silence can blow away the fog of influence to reveal our deepest seeds of sensation and imagination. One would believe that no sound stimulation would mean no impressions but the opposite may be true. To pull from our own source and construct whatever foundation may be lurking is to dig up our innovative intuition. Meditate on your technique or sound to further build and succeed them.

Life and its entire intricate situation can weigh heavily on our backs. The flow of catastrophic events and the sense of our own impending doom have an influence that drown our perspectives to depths only a skilled perceiver can translate into an observable art. Embrace being face-to-face with your own darkness and cynicism. Finding the core of what drives so many to a paralyzing emotion can be used as a reflection, mirroring and recognizing our hidden disasters. As artist, we have opportunities to cut open our own sense of demise and tragedies to therapeutically explain them through song, picture, film and story. When we cut through the smoke of depressions, our scope into sharing what is within remains the tool that grants all other participants of the same heartache the sense of community within.

As an artist, performer or anyone, we are easy to be bashful with advancing a drastic technical or expressive move. That bashful anxiety may stem from the fear of failing. The fear of being humbled after entering a dojo, the fear of butchering a vocal phrase that's new and foreign are both small situations that represent the great disabler of our evolving skill sets. The obstacle of fear is a movable and breakable force. Letting go of the self-disposition towards the unknown may help in allowing ourselves to advance and break the outer wall of our mind in facing a new level. Letting go of how you feel once embarrassed, ridiculed or unsuccessful will fuel the control of our direction. The analogy of digging your own trench while building the physical body to the point of being able to overcome and scale the walls to climb up and out is an idea that runs parallel to the potential of our rolling ambitions, dreams and make-up of character.

The engine that drives our daily moments and steers much of life's outcomes can be said to be fueled by motives and a personal ethos. The way we can view ourselves, our relationships and the world can muster up many states of mind that fight to be expressed. As artists, our mental space can weigh like an anaconda around our shoulders. What can lighten the load is to monitor how we feel and act upon these gripping episodes of negative and positive trials. Recognize when you're at the core of a personal transformation or overwhelming emotion and grab the pen, the brush, any instrument of choice and make the attempt to translate yourself. Boil the happiness, fear and confusions to the bare element. This doesn't mean the articulation you produce through your abilities has to or will reflect what you feel. Your emotional state can churn the engines of action but isn't exclusive to creating something reflective of the initial thought. Use the fears towards death to mold an expression that displays an appreciation for life. Look into your sensation of loss and bare the heart of turmoil to possibly reconstruct yourself through self-realizing the issue. Keeping tabs on where we are emotionally, as difficult as it is at times, will serve you as your greatest ally in continuing your creative endeavors and keeping the results bounded to sincerity.

Our thoughts on a particular matter, at times, can be compared to when a scope magnifies certain specifics to great volume. The quality and drive to view a project with great attention to detail may aid in the elusively progressive undertone that we may choose to execute within a tune. The understanding of technique behind moving a story musically at times can propel it under the dedication of tedious analysis. The descent into the desire of luring the audience's ear can open a panoramic view to the minute tonal and percussive movements that have towering effects. Think of the ringing sound on a ride bell to the splash of a high hat resolving with the crash of a china cymbal. Think of the bass drum kick on the beats of 1 and 3 in a measure and then having the kick drum sync up with specific rhythmic movements in the guitar riff. Lastly, expand and ascend in the last few measures of a section with the kick on every 16th note while sustaining the same guitar progression. These and countless other simple examples can be the major subtleties in the twisting maze you guide the listener when implementing a song that make a colossal difference. Our attention to detail can be further implemented as "intention in detail." In the way the protagonist in a story reveals herself through precise specifics that presume character insight, is the same in how songs reveal their provoking expression through minuscule instrumental changes.

Ruthless is a word that can be taken as perceptually alarming. But the attitude can have an energy that carries a heavy load of positive action. Ambition toward the pursuit of personal purpose should be pushed with the position like that of a wolf concerning an enemy. Conviction in the attack from the productive side of yourself possesses the forte to spearhead the stumbling around your obstacles, your doubtful thought. The wolf commits to the idea that there will be no potential distraction or resistance to the vicious moment at hand. She knows her survival is the only option as her senses transform and elevate. She battles to the death as we should in the fight against our hallucinations, worries and thoughts that demobilize our self-evolution. Be ruthless like the wolf. Bare your teeth at yourself. Breathe into the face of your fear and carry all your prospects past the threshold that opposes you. Be ruthless to the pursuit of balance in all your priorities, your happiness.

A notion that many creative creatures hold about their best work entails that the quality and result are majorly dictated by the inspiration sprung through personal calamities and distress. The chaos in our lives can make for such fertile ground in the jungle of topics. We tend to hyper focus on our situations when the lows of our lives are entangled with a chocking grip. And in typical fashion we release ourselves therapeutically in expressing the darkness throughout our art. The handicap in this idea lies in the assumption that peak and consistent flow of creativity will be exhausted if we're not in a state of stress. It's a convincing veil when we feel that the level of insight and depth will be lost by the hand of our own recovery and happiness. The act of creating the expression, some would believe, is a leap toward survival, a mechanism that's drawn on by the need for emotional reclamation. If we feel self-gratified after writing our passages, painting our canvas, or writing a song, should that not be the insight to the slant we should take to stay in that mode of thinking? Indulge in other interactions and practices that reinforce the positive evolution of your self-awareness. Move into the world that peaks through achievements and discover your productivity with a more content state of mind. Though the tone of our expressions may change, it's a welcomed price to pay for snapping the chains from the slavery of our illusionary destructive motivation.

Technique

There are tactics in song construction that can be looked at as a type of parlor trick. A goal of certain songs is to keep the listener compelled and on track with the sense of familiarity using foreshadowing techniques. Every element of a section whether it be the verse, climb, chorus, A, B, or C can be modified to be utilized again later in the structure as a transition or whole new passage. The most minuscule change can give the segment its reason to come back around or to transform identity all together.

Vocal melodies can be the initial conductor towards the music beneath it. A deceptive but refreshing tactic can be used with a well formatted melody. Take the chorus blue prints for example. If you set up an open, uncongested space musically for the vocal line, then a modulation of the progression can replace the old phrases but retain the same melody. You can hear the familiar chorus vocals moving along new chords or picking patterns that now accompany. For the modification to work easier the progressions may need to stay within the boundaries of the previous key signature or mode. Stylistically, this can be open to an endless amount of approaches. Syncing the melody and the music at certain pulses in the measure is a difficult angle to this approach but effective in its auditory foreplay.

There's an expression called "fishing" in the slang of music terms. Teachers describe it as wasteful moments searching for music ideas with a theory-less mind. A belief in which, it is not constructive to try and see in the darkness. But ask any fisherman and they will say it is not about the fish at the end of the line but the experience of fishing that brings one to love fishing. "Fishing" instrumentally can be an improvisation that trains the mind and eyes about the spaces between the theoretical lines. Explore the unknown territory and give yourself the experience of cringing at the unwelcomed, accidental sounds. Through all the mishaps in your investigation, you may stumble onto a gem of an idea that may never have been reached if an orthodox, theoretical approach was implemented. Cut down and through all the shrubs to arrive at your destination rather than follow the quick road. It may be a better way.

At the core of all music there is an attribute that innately pulls at the listening ear in a wide range of levels. This characteristic is called the line of tension aspect. Like a needle on a polygraph, there is a mental line that travels as a song unfolds through the ears. To recognize this line as a composer is an insight that is a great advantage towards one's personal variety of storytelling through song. This line can range from the form of an arch similar to the path of an arrow to the complex and precise valleys in the teeth of a key. Recognize the relationship between the pulling and holding of an arrow and its release. They are essential to transmitting the drama of your message. In the end, the point should pierce its target.

A simple yet effective way to link varies songs, if you're engineering a concept or multi-passage unit, is to reuse a section by disguising it with theatrical or stylistic changes. Try using the climb of one song as a segue point of another's bridge. Decorate the progression in accordance to the new key signature by infusing possibly a half time feel, triplet time or manipulating the riff by only exposing small phrases of the progression. This method has many unpredictable and subtle options. Use this strategy as a mental rope that pulls the listener back to whatever chosen lyrical or sonic theme you've initiated. It will come across as new but still tug at a memory reminiscent of something familiar.

A wonderful way to build tension and launch a listener up the peak of release can be in the use of a phrase that begins very abstract, absent of instrumental layers and textures. In the climb to a chorus or any central plateau, experiment with starting off setting the pulse and rhythm with only the drums and bass. Stripping down the music to its skeletal frame can allow a patient process of gradually introducing layers of instrumentation plus vocals.

Put yourself in the sandals of a snake charmer of rhythm. Sway the serpent to a 6/8 feel and as the black diamond rises, demand its attention. A guitar riff can have many emotional implications as life bites at our hearts. Instincts plant themselves in the face of our filters to dismantle the mechanism that dilutes our most accurate and honest thought. It allows for insight to be transformed into music through the instrumental sword of our choice. Placing the scope of our attention on hope, happiness or rage, has potential to fire up the techniques that help interpret the inner strength and turmoil's that grind us. As musicians we work tirelessly on the understanding of the technical approach. But like any fight, without heart, the fists will never plant themselves onto their target. A notable translation for an intense, attention grabbing groove is the 6/8 feel at a forceful pace. Accented by the heavy attack of an electric guitar can be a recipe for a great barreling train of aggressive thought. It can be a challenge grappling this mode of writing on guitar but once executed, even at a novice level, a new door of expression has been unlocked. Channel the emotion that serves you in the moment and summon it from the pool of serpents. Let your presence and abilities be known to the snake of rhythm and command the purity of its nature.

If you enjoy and have the resources to write parallel guitar passages, this next idea may add a textural component to your compositional skill. There are moments when the rhythm guitars have opportunities to venture off and accentuate the other. As one side of the sound spectrum plays the riff which usually consists of chords played on a lower register. The phrase allows for the backdrop that, depending on the chosen notes, brings about the modal and moody identity of the second riff. The second riff is the emphasis here. It's most common to write out a lead melody within the higher registers underneath its' accenting counterpart which is the heavier of the two riffs. Usually these two interact in a section that repeats. Here is where we should think about progressing the lead melody to change as the phrase repeats.

Wrapping up a song can be at times the most difficult or simple move of the process. Often times the end consists of one last chorus. But even the chorus can be slightly modified to emphasize the end. Resolve it with some attraction to help keep the listener attached all through segments end. Once the phrase has been played through the first time, come back around and arrange a harmony line parallel to your original vocal line. Introducing a whole new counter vocal melody that uses a call and response with certain words can add that useful flair too. One of the more prominent techniques involves changing the percussion. Cutting the pulse into a halftime feel drastically manipulates how the listener takes in that phrase as opposed what they have grown accustomed to previously.

For anyone who likes to embark through the mental maze of constructing an exceptionally longer song, this small tip may reveal access to one way of achieving it. Never mind the countless maneuvers that can be applied in and around your first verse, climb, chorus etc. The main direction for this example heads inside the middle or bridge section of your song. The idea is to slip a smaller song structure within the larger one. Typically as we move past our second chorus, we move into the bridge that can consist of listening through two or three passages until we reach the wrap up or ending of the tune. Use the section immediately after the second chorus to tie all the beginning content with what we can call the mini song, which now identifies itself as the bridge. Think of your verse, climb and chorus but in a very condensed way. Shorten all their lengths and play with opposing keys or modes when constructing all the pieces. It shouldn't feel like its stepping past its retention boundaries. There should still be a sense of riding the momentum through the story.

❀

Reflections

The genesis to the emotional bondage I have with music started when my mind would vicariously play out moments of triumph fueled by the artists in the headphones Id sit with. The absence of a few essential figures that usually aid in a child's confidence and self-definition spiraled my need to latch onto anything that resembled a guide. Music, during a lot of the private moments, allowed me to live out the revenge towards my suppressors, pursue an adolescent love or feel exhilarated by being on stage and devouring the energy by the hand of my musicianship. My self-belief as a child was fragile early on but just pretending that I had control and the capability of overcoming my melodramas was transformative. The impressions would slowly cross over from mental daydreaming to real world motion. The domain in which my continually developing securities flourished, gradually cascading over and onto my interactions in my later years. It seemed that I needed to play out the victories within first. The hopelessness and confusion in matters of love, guidance and identity were gradually fashioned by one of the most influential therapies available to me. Boys fantasize of many things and I strictly used the pill of music to send me down the wormhole towards, I believe, the fundamentals of an introverted self-seeking pathfinder.

There's a feature to many different disciplines and practices that I find become a catalyst toward a frightening but beneficial state of mind. By the process of studying, creating and enjoying the idea of music, it had forced me to shut out many of my distractions. I had found myself comfortable in isolation but anxious from the amplified thoughts about who I was and the illusions that catered to my paranoia. It seemed to go hand in hand that solitary creativity would induce a curiosity into deeper parts of my thinking. I wanted to know more about my anger, my depression, my lack of self-worth, oppose to wandering on the crust of awareness and not mining through the roots. The repetition of swimming in my headspace, finding the substance worthy of a song, and reliving the affliction to better understand it had brought me to then, silence my mind. I pondered alone grinding away at my craft for so long that it began to stir the soup of my ambiguity. The solitude required in the hyper focus towards the reflective qualities of songwriting had maneuvered me into a reflective mode of meditation and mindful training. I believe it's a tremendous attribute to focus on the moment to moment activities in our environment. If music hadn't ripped me away from the turbulent crossroads that entangled my impressionable judgments, life with many of its exaggerations and temporary hiccups would have been magnified to a debilitating handicap.

There's a rampant beast that hunts in the field of frequencies that's identified as the human perception. It devours the ideas of identity by attaching the sense of who we are to an external mechanism or process. That was the poison I had added to a muse that's void of all discrimination. Like the code of a novice samurai, I took the pursuit of music as an extension of my convictions, willpower and integrity. I had taken every struggling moment against personal progress as an offence to my new found permitted addiction. My emotional attachment to the idea of developing myself away from all the hindering inadequacies in my character by mastering the daunting summit of music was an inevitable dangerous game. It may be true that in facing the complexities of any skills based endeavor, we uproot the hidden or weaker parts of our capabilities by being humbled and pushing through. But to use that path as a crutch for a crippled identity, breaks you when all you see in the reflection is an artist and not the vast creature of potential. I had submerged so much of my energy in a self-identifying way that if I wasn't constantly working towards my greater goals I became dissatisfied with life and the countless riches that encompass it. When songs started to come less seldom and the more that time slipped away from any momentum in my pursuits, the deeper the terror would sink in the value of myself. It became very difficult to engage and enjoy the daily interactions with the feeling that my obsession had left me with a list of unfulfilled external accomplishments. Luckily, the interests of understanding my perception and feeding the curiosity of the mind, diverted the toxic illusion I had incased myself with. But the experiences I gained in the discipline I had exerted, made it that much easier to know the truth that I was capable of many other pursuits whether it be mental or physical. And as I recognized the bitterness towards my supposed shortcomings, fueled by misread dedication, I became free to face the distortion of who I had become. The reality was that I was an apprehensive, insecure, overcompensating child finding his way through the self-testing dimensions of music and study. Recognizing this took an incredible load of pressure off my shoulders. I became emancipated not only to see the falsehood in the grand notion but to use my abilities I had sharpened as a musician to take on my many other voices of creativity with vitality. Stepping outside of that screaming fixation with a little more objectivity allowed me to shine a light on what had happened. And in using music as a bridge, I walked away from my old externally based identity and exposed the confidence that was kidnapped so long ago.

The catharsis that music invokes now is much more of a sparring match between a sensei and her student for me. I can step on the dojo floor tight and rusty or aggressively focused. There's a message to be deeply humbled by that amuses the many skills and strengths of the motivated self. It was such a foreign feeling neglecting the daily habits of the anxiety fueled practice sessions. The guilt would seem to be increased in the idea that I needed to create something not to exercise a mental muscle but to gain a step towards notoriety or "success". For a time I felt ashamed for how much of my efforts seemed to be in vain. But the liberation that exuberated once I held the guitar again and opened a new recording session was the peace I thought was only attributed to a certain level of recognition. These new moments of inspiration became enveloped in a much more profound personal cloud. I was still able to refine the tools I had worked ruthlessly to acquire. The patience, the observance and creative molding it takes to satisfy ones productivity in writing music are the flags, I believe, that help guide our many other pursuits and relationships. The testing and manifestation of my attributes through the instruments became the alchemy to my inner peace. The practice of it all is much different now. The lassoing of the muse has transformed into a meditation that flexes the abilities of the person I've always been, separate of the musician.

There was something profound that revealed itself to me on a personal level. From years of disbelief which transformed into a healthier self-awareness, to an obsession that evolved into a mental meditation, music had maneuvered me to a space of mindful balance. I had certainly benefited from the years of commitment with the experiences that shaped my outlook. But when all was said and done, the reality that I had succumb to was that I had neglected the many other facets of my life. Tunnel vision, reinforced with a linear way of thinking, I believe, is a sure win for obtaining most subjective goals. But with the bridges burned and the experiences lost, I had become my most painful sign of an unbalanced priority. That's why it's important to have our art, our hobbies, our professions, our discipline or any pursuit, bring our sight inward and hitchhike back to a mode of reflection. I needed to understand the origins of why this psychological ride spiraled so recklessly for so long. That's an incredible wave to swim into. It knocks your breath and presses terror into the drowning mind. My delusion came from the misconception that I was a product of external events that in turn pushed the internal drive onto external needs. If my emotions damaged easily due to an earlier observation of patronizing or belittling altercations then my yearning for worthiness was perused by vicarious means. This would become the template to much of why I invested so much of my identity in my achievements and not my convictions. I would also mimic the false persona that was reinforced by the demeaning and harsh message aggressively conditioned into me. The deception that the world's lack of belief in you can be powerful enough to convince you that it speaks the gospel. The abuse came from the daunting amount of self-scolding that I pounded myself with. The betrayal I felt came from the feeling that I had ran away from the fettered child which held my absolute potential. Death came from when I truly vanquished the spell that blindfolded the sight to my circumstance and killed the automation I once was. Lawless was the violence I gave this tumor in my psychology. Without these turn of events that later on would be cherry picked into reflective expressions, I would have never been drawn to music in the way that I was, which guided me to understand and recognize my own entrapment. When a creative practice acts as a weapon that strikes down and dismantles the impressed toxins of our perception, it's a difficult task to not regard that practice as the almighty priority. The balance between engaging in all of my ambitions and allowing the many other experiences and lessons began once I had felt the recovery from the long journey of my complex. I had somehow filled the trenches in my character by flooding them with the current that flows at the peak of my creative moments. And at this peak I feel accurate, powerful, reflective, fulfilled and calm. Luckily the recent bitterness over my exhausted energy, I believe, became the signal for the end. Through the hard realization that specific curtains of opportunity had shut behind me, my discipline had revealed a purpose in its design. My music had expelled most if not all its core philosophy unto me. I had grasped advantage and failure, focus and conviction, adversity and companionship, compromise and defiance, including an innumerable account of experiences. The crutch I had leaned on for so long had finally aided in healing my wounds. When I began exploring the dimensions of music it was to build a persona, empty of all fragile and inadequate psychological traits. Who knew that music with a hint of resilient survival would water the seeds of character to bloom a life void of any persona at all? My very personal path has had many levels of experimentation that forced me to throw caution and fear to the wind. Engulf yourself in anything that demands your multifaceted attention. Study and experience as many physical, mental and emotional obligations and milestones. They will uproot the nature and importance of who you are at the densest level, only to become immovable and boundless toward equilibrium in ourselves and gratitude for all we love.

Special Thanks

Thank you to my family and friends for allowing me to mimic some of their great standards of character and creativity.

Thank you to the teachers who taught me how to locate and uncover the deepest jewels of honesty and humility beneath my resistance.

For more activity from Harry visit

www.zenstrings.webs.com

www.momentumunderground.podbean.com

(Audio Podcast)

www.youtube.com/user/harrymoraga

(Video Podcast)

www.facebook.com/harry.moraga

Twitter@HarryMoraga

www.soundcloud.com/harry-moraga

Refer to the zenstrings.webs.com domain for original music that contains examples of the techniques discussed in chapter 2.

Refer to **www.youtube.com/user/zenstringsbook** for an online video companion to many of the books excerpts .Enjoy!

ZEN STRINGS

ZEN STRINGS

ZEN STRINGS   Page 81

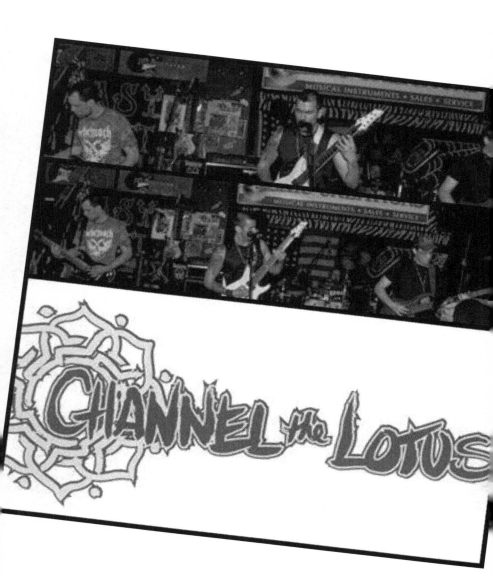

ZEN STRINGS

Dedicated to Shanna

"Sometimes that mountain you've been climbing is just a grain of sand. And what you have been searching for forever is in your hands."

Proof

Made in the USA
Charleston, SC
27 August 2015